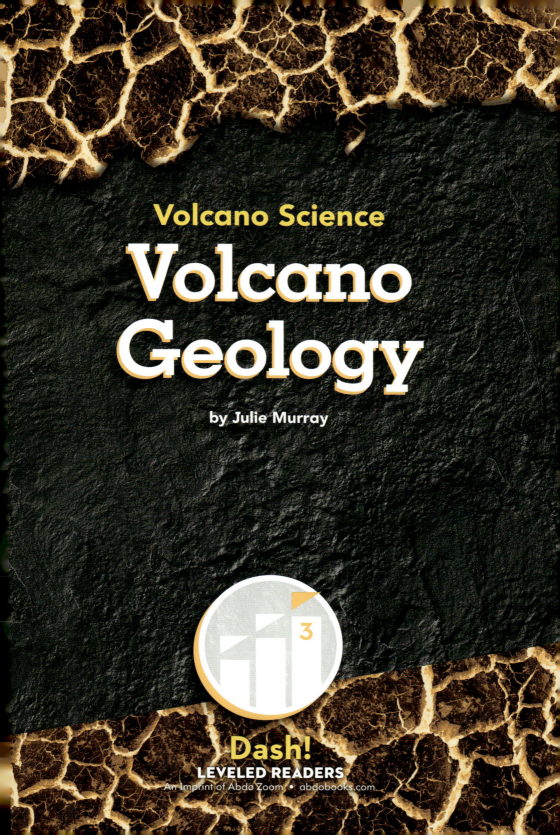

Volcano Science

Volcano Geology

by Julie Murray

Dash!
LEVELED READERS

Level 1 – Beginning
Short and simple sentences with familiar words or patterns for children who are beginning to understand how letters and sounds go together.

Level 2 – Emerging
Longer words and sentences with more complex language patterns for readers who are practicing common words and letter sounds.

Level 3 – Transitional
More developed language and vocabulary for readers who are becoming more independent.

THIS BOOK CONTAINS RECYCLED MATERIALS

abdobooks.com

Published by Abdo Zoom, a division of ABDO, PO Box 398166, Minneapolis, Minnesota 55439. Copyright © 2023 by Abdo Consulting Group, Inc. International copyrights reserved in all countries. No part of this book may be reproduced in any form without written permission from the publisher. Dash!™ is a trademark and logo of Abdo Zoom.

Printed in the United States of America, North Mankato, Minnesota.
052022
092022

Photo Credits: Alamy, Getty Images, Science Source, Shutterstock
Production Contributors: Kenny Abdo, Jennie Forsberg, Grace Hansen, John Hansen
Design Contributors: Candice Keimig, Neil Klinepier

Library of Congress Control Number: 2021950297

Publisher's Cataloging in Publication Data

Names: Murray, Julie, author.
Title: Volcano geology / by Julie Murray.
Description: Minneapolis, Minnesota : Abdo Zoom, 2023 | Series: Volcano science | Includes online resources and index.
Identifiers: ISBN 9781098228422 (lib. bdg.) | ISBN 9781098229269 (ebook) | ISBN 9781098229689 (Read-to-Me ebook)
Subjects: LCSH: Volcanoes--Juvenile literature. | Geology--Juvenile literature. | Volcanism--Juvenile literature. | Physical geography--Juvenile literature.
Classification: DDC 551.21--dc23

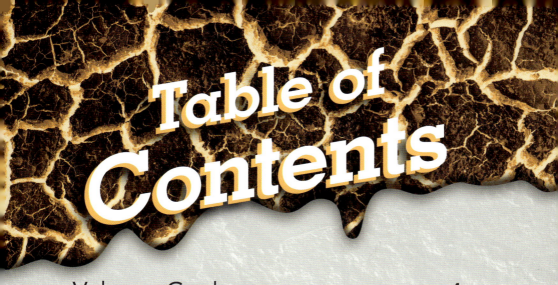

Table of Contents

Volcano Geology 4

How Volcanoes Form 8

Igneous Rocks 20

More Volcano Facts 22

Glossary 23

Index 24

Online Resources 24

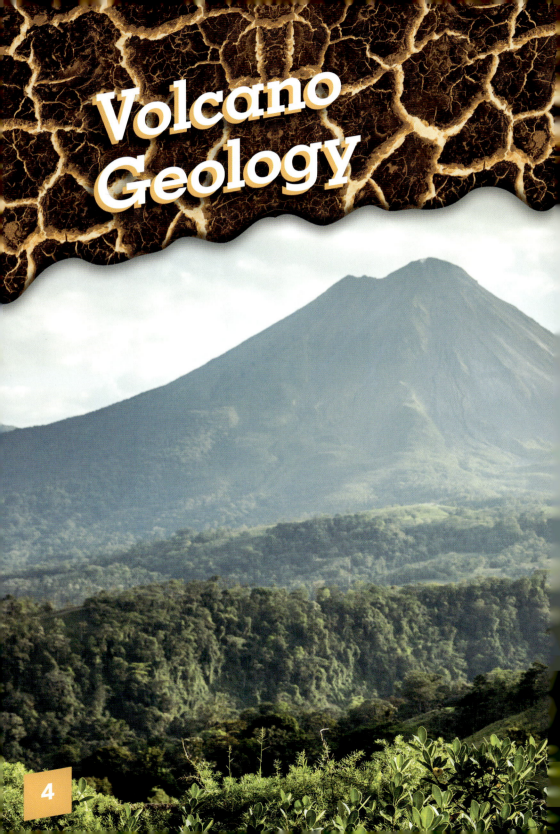

Volcano Geology

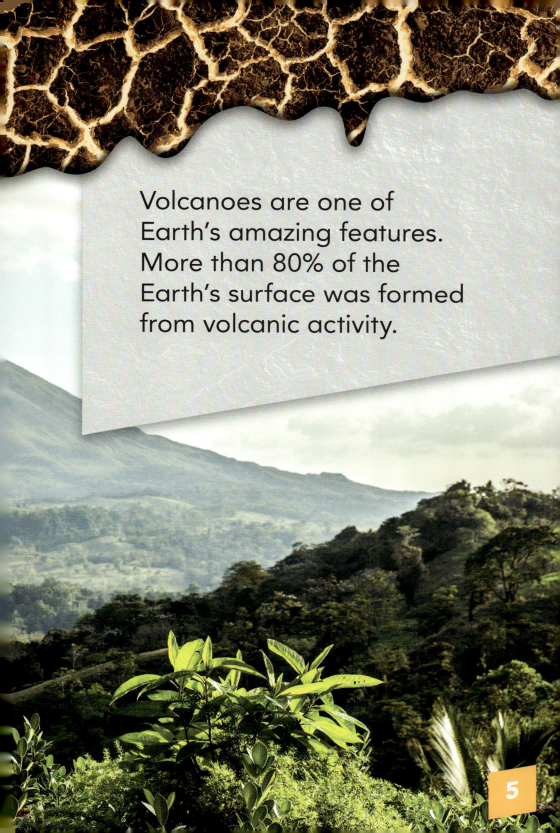

Volcanoes are one of Earth's amazing features. More than 80% of the Earth's surface was formed from volcanic activity.

A volcano is an opening in the Earth's surface. Magma, ash, and gases escape from this opening during a volcanic eruption.

How Volcanoes Form

The Earth is made up of four layers. The inner core is at the center. Next is the outer core. The mantle is the third layer. The crust is the outer layer.

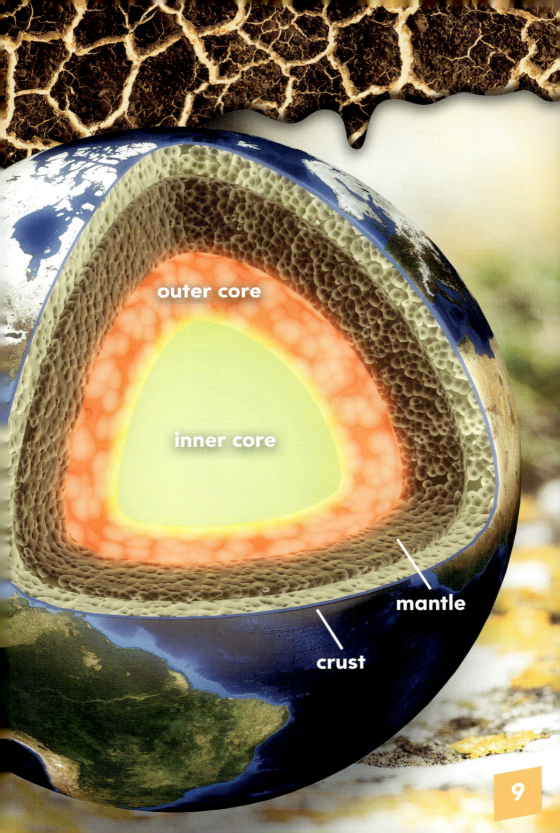

Earth's crust is made up of **tectonic plates**. These plates move and **collide**. Their movement is what causes volcanoes to form and erupt. This can happen in different ways.

When plates **collide**, one slides on top and the other is pushed down. This creates heat and **pressure** deep in the Earth. Magma moves toward the surface, causing an eruption.

The plates can also move away from each other. In this case, magma fills in the space. It again rises to the surface.

14

Hot spots also help volcanoes form. Streams of hot magma rise to the surface because it is so hot. Magma pushes through cracks in the crust.

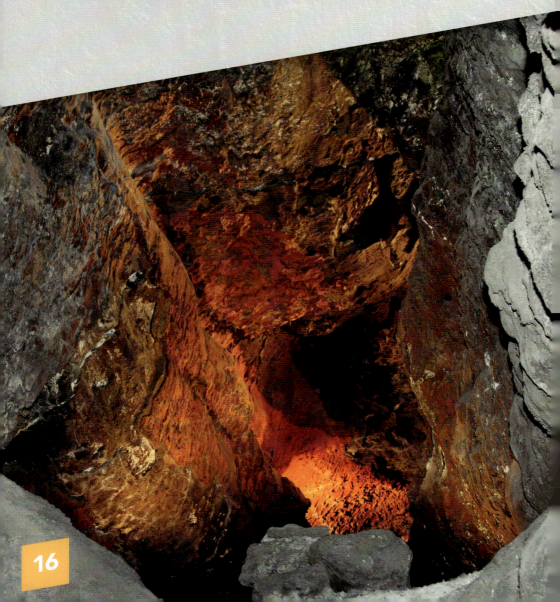

After an eruption, the lava and **debris** harden as they cool forming new rock.

Over time, volcanoes can grow bigger and bigger. Sometimes they lose height after an eruption. Their shapes are constantly changing.

Igneous Rocks

Igneous rocks form from cooling magma. Some form just below the surface where magma cools over thousands of years. These rocks are often very large.

Granite and peridotite form below ground

Pumice and obsidian form above ground

Igneous rock can also form above ground where lava cools much faster. These rocks can have lots of holes or look like glass.

More Volcano Facts

- The word "volcano" comes from the Roman god of fire, Vulcan.

- About 800 million people live within what's called the "danger range" of an active volcano.

- The only rock that can float is pumice rock, which forms above ground from quick-cooling lava after an explosive eruption.

- Yellowstone in Wyoming is a supervolcano that last erupted 70,000 years ago.

- Jupiter's moon Io is the most active volcanic area in our **solar system** with about 400 active volcanoes.

Glossary

collide – to strike or bump into one another with force.

debris – scattered pieces left after something has been destroyed.

hot spot – in geology, an area on Earth over a mantle plume or an area under the Earth's crust where magma is hotter than the surrounding magma. The magma plume causes melting and thinning of the rocky crust and widespread volcanic activity.

pressure – a steady force upon a surface.

solar system – our Sun, its eight planets and their moons, and all other bodies that travel around the Sun.

tectonic plate – one of the plate-like segments of the Earth's crust and upper mantle. The plates form the outer shell of the planet. They move very slowly. Where the plates meet each other, their movement can cause or play a part in the eruption of volcanoes, the building of mountains, and earthquakes.

Index

ash 6

Earth's layers 8, 11, 12

eruptions 6, 11, 12, 18, 19

gases 6

igneous rock 20, 21

lava 18, 21

magma 6, 12, 14, 16

tectonic plates 11, 12, 14, 16

Online Resources

Booklinks NONFICTION NETWORK
FREE! ONLINE NONFICTION RESOURCES

To learn more about volcano geology, please visit **abdobooklinks.com** or scan this QR code. These links are routinely monitored and updated to provide the most current information available.